STORMS 2

Tales of Extreme Weather Events in Minnesota

By Sheri O'Meara

the *Minnesota* series

150 YEARS
of STATEHOOD
1858 · 2008

Welcome to *Storms 2*

In *Storms 2*, the fourth book in The Minnesota Series, you'll find stories and rare photographs about more major weather events in Minnesota. Inside, look back on and learn about storms that affected our lives and our state. Previous books in the series include *Storms!*, *Music Legends* and *Media Tales*. Coming up next: *Famous Crimes*. Pick up books at retailers across the state or order online at www.minnesotaseries.com. Enjoy *Storms 2!*

Author **Sheri O'Meara**
Design and Layout **Phil Tippin**
Proofreader **Marsha Kitchel**
Web Consultant **Risdall Advertising, New Brighton, Minn.**
Printing **Bang Printing, Brainerd, Minn.**
Publishers **D Media: Debra Gustafson Decker, Dale Decker**

©2007 by D Media Inc., 4507 Lakeview Dr., Minneapolis, MN 55424.
(952) 926-3950. dmedia@juno.com. www.minnesotaseries.com.
Books available at www.minnesotaseries.com

ISBN 9780978795641

Library of Congress Control Number: 2007938012

RISDALL ADVERTISING AGENCY

To donate to the Red Cross for 35W bridge collapse relief or to funds to help 2007 southeastern Minnesota flood victims, please go to www.redcrosstc.org.

Cover photos courtesy NSSL

Contents

Foreword

As Minnesotans, we pride ourselves on our endurance and tolerance to our long, cold winters and hot, muggy summers. We're able to brag about the recent extreme we endured. It's almost the stuff of legends, like Paul Bunyan and Babe the Blue Ox. The difference, of course, is that our extreme weather, and hence, extreme climate, is a real-life adventure.

This is a land of extremes. It's not coincidental. Like so many things, it's all about location, location, location! We have the ideal setup for temperature extremes. This leads to extraordinarily wild weather as a result. There are few modifiers to our climate. There are no tall mountains to block dense cold, ground-hugging air nor an enormous body of water (comparable to an ocean) to quench the thirst of a hot, dry air plume. This gives us our spectrum of temperature records from -60 F to +114 F.

All this accumulates to produce periodic droughts, floods, blizzards, tornadoes and much, much more. Events that we carry in our memory. Experiences that don't just affect us or are observed by us but become our collective being and turn us into a state of weather junkies.

In this, the second *Storms* book in the Minnesota Series, remember with me, these tales of extreme weather.

Sven Sundgaard, Meteorologist, KARE-11, Minneapolis-St. Paul

The 1930s Dust Bowl
Drought and Black Blizzards

Now the wind grew strong and hard, it worked at the rain crust in the cornfields. Little by little the sky was darkened by the mixing dust, and the wind fell over the earth, loosened the dust and carried it away.
　　　　　　　　　　　　—*The Grapes of Wrath*, 1939, by John Steinbeck

Of all the blizzards, tornadoes, rainstorms and floods Minnesotans have battled, the Dust Bowl reigns as the most devastating weather event to hit the state. As fields dried up and began to blow away in the 1930s, the extreme drought and "black blizzards" spawned quiet but profound human suffering that became a way of life for a generation.

It is easy to think of the Dust Bowl as exclusively a southern and central plains event: Haunting photographs and popular literature from the era have told us that hundreds of thousands of desperate people from Oklahoma, Texas, Arkansas and Missouri abandoned homes and migrated west, in search of jobs and survival. But when the Minnesota State Climatology Office asked Minnesota's climate experts to select the Most Significant Minnesota Weather Event of the 20th Century, they didn't choose a typically Minnesotan storm like a blizzard. The pundits named the Dust Bowl.

According to the climatology office: "Perhaps the most devastating weather-driven event in American history, the drought of the 1920s and 1930s significantly impacted Minnesota's economic, social and natural landscapes.

A combination of cutworms and heat has destroyed the corn on this farm, five miles east of Appleton. (photo: Minnesota Historical Society)

Abnormally dry and hot growing season weather throughout the better part of two decades turned Minnesota farm fields to dust and small lakes into muddy ponds. The parched soil was easily taken up by strong winds, often turning day into night. The drought peaked with the heat of the summer of 1936, setting many high-temperature records that still stand today."

The Dust Bowl coincided with the Great Depression. But the trouble didn't come crashing down all at once when the stock market collapsed in 1929. In Minnesota, the drought began in 1921, state climatologists say, though the severe drought alone was not solely responsible for the dust storms. Years of "land misuse" while farming contributed to the damage. The land had been broken by repeated plowing, and depleted of its nutrients by planting and replanting. It was the same across the plains. "When the high wartime prices collapsed in the early-1920s, plainsmen broke more sod (largely with the newly adopted one-way disc plow) in order to plant more wheat to offset the economic loss which low prices caused," according to the paper "DUST BOWL: Drought, Erosion and Despair on the Southern Great Plains" by R. Douglas Hurt. "New technology, war and depressed prices stimulated Great Plains farmers to break 32 million acres of sod between 1909 and 1929 for new wheat lands. … At this time Great Plains farmers gave little thought to the protection of the soil. … Furthermore, continued cultivation pulverized the soil and made it susceptible to wind erosion."

For nearly two decades in Minnesota, the unrelenting sun and drought dried up the soil, which turned to dust, and blew away.

"The first sign of trouble surfaced in the late-'20s, when crop prices began to drop and the first of the area banks closed," according to a 1999 *Star Tribune* story recalling the hard decades in southern Minnesota. "The Great Depression of the 1930s hit the farmers in the Midwest especially hard, and Redwood County in southwestern Minnesota was no exception. Banks failed, crop prices collapsed and hard-working families were forced to the streets and shelters in search of food and clothing. In Redwood County, the hardships were documented weekly in the *Redwood Falls Gazette*. Half-page to full-page ads publicizing farm foreclosure auctions appeared regularly. In 1931, 43 farms in the county sold at mortgage sales. In 1932, it jumped to 126. In 1933, 91 were sold off."

The Dust Bowl is considered to be the most extreme drought and longest in duration of recorded history. According to "History of Drought in the Northern Plains," a paper by Red River Basin Board's Hydrology Team, the drought "affected two-thirds of the United States while producing a 40 percent reduction in corn and wheat yields. The biggest enemy of agriculturists was the strong winds out of the west and southwest. Dry, sandy topsoil was blown away by 'dusters' and 'black blizzards' and deposited as drifts in feed stacks. Cattle died from starvation and suffocation as dust covered pastureland. Between 1930 and 1934 alone there was an estimated $5 billion loss in agriculture. Lake Michigan and Huron were also measured to be at their all-time lowest levels during the late 1930s."

Nationally, there were said to be four separate droughts during the Dust Bowl years: 1930-31, 1934, 1936 and

1939-40. One followed the other in such rapid succession that regions never got a chance to recover.

In 1931, National Weather Service recorders in Milan in western Minnesota recorded 73 days without precipitation, and by then, the income of the Minnesota dairy industry had fallen to 25 percent of its former level. But hard times in Minnesota were not limited to farms in those years: "Unemployment increased alarmingly. Its severity was underlined in the fall of 1932, when 70 percent of the Minnesota Iron Range workers were jobless," according to the book *Minnesota: A History of the State.*

In 1933, the legislature passed an emergency law stopping farm foreclosure sales. By the time Franklin Delano Roosevelt took office in 1933, the country was in desperate straits. FDR declared a four-day bank holiday, and Congress initiated the Emergency Banking Act of 1933, attempting to stabilize the banking industry. Government programs were launched to restore the ecologic balance, including forming the Soil Conservation Service, now the Natural Resources Conservation Service. But it would be many years before the programs would have an effect on the damaged land.

Meanwhile, the dust blew.

According to the *Minnesota Weather Almanac:* "On November 11 and 12, 1933, a severe dust storm struck in Minnesota's southern and central counties, sending visibility to near zero; the observer at Redwood Falls in Redwood county called it the worst dust storm in the city's history."

It's difficult for many modern Minnesotans to understand dust storms as common occurrences in this

state. Lawrence Schaub, who was a small boy on a farm
near Glenwood during the Dust Bowl, recalls in his journal,
archived by the Minnesota Historical Society:

"Dust storms were quite frequent and were a
frightening thing to see. ... When a dust storm moved into
our area you could see this huge black cloud of dust coming
right at us. We always ran into the house when we saw this
cloud coming. When the storm hit our farm, the sun would
dim considerably and we would barely be able to see our barn,
which was about 300 feet from our house. At times it would
become so dark inside our house we would light the lanterns.
... No one went out of the house during these storms unless
it was absolutely necessary. My older brothers would place
handkerchiefs over their nose and mouth in the event that
they had to tend to the livestock. ... You could hear the wind
howling outside and the dust and dirt blowing through the
windows. During these storms, dust would get inside the house
and cover everything in there. ..."

Dust piled up. Everywhere. Even the most persnickety
housekeeper could not keep it away. It's clear John Steinbeck
wrote from true Dust Bowl experience in *The Grapes of Wrath*:
"Houses were shut tight, and cloth wedged around doors and
windows, but the dust came in so thinly that it could not be
seen in the air, and it settled like pollen on the chairs and
tables, on the dishes."

One entrepreneur saw a rare opportunity: "After the
ceilings of two Dodge City homes collapsed from the weight of
accumulated dust in the attic, one enterprising man obtained
an oversized carpet sweeper and went into the attic-cleaning

business," reports "DUST BOWL: Drought, Erosion, and Despair on the Southern Great Plains."

Schaub's journal further notes a sad condition that other Minnesota reports of the era confirm: "Livestock suffered terribly during this time. It is hard to believe now, but they would eat just about anything, including thistles and even tumbleweeds."

In 1934, nearly one-third of the working population of Duluth was unemployed, and dust storms multiplied nationally. By 1934, it was estimated that 100 million acres of farmland had lost all or most of the topsoil to the winds. Drought covered more than 75 percent of the country, affecting 27 states severely. According to Wikipedia, "On May 11, 1934, a strong two-day dust storm removed massive amounts of Great Plains topsoil in one of the worst such storms of the Dust Bowl. The dust clouds blew all the way to Chicago, where filth fell like snow, dumping the equivalent of four pounds of debris per person on the city. Several days later, the same storm reached cities in the east, such as Buffalo, Boston, New York City, and Washington, D.C. That winter, red snow fell on New England."

On April 14, 1935, a day that came to be known as "Black Sunday," the worst black blizzard of the Dust Bowl rolled in. The storm engulfed Stratford, Texas, and actually suffocated some residents. The Dust Bowl got its name the next day, when Robert Geiger, a reporter for the Associated Press, wrote: "Three little words achingly familiar on a Western farmer's tongue, rule life in the dust bowl of the continent—if it rains." The term stuck.

The following month, 200 World War I veterans—workers with the new federal Civilian Conservation Corps—came to Sibley State Park in Kandiyohi County, and for the next three years they planted 10,000 trees, installed a water system and built roads and trails. The New Deal was under way in Minnesota.

By this time, without vegetation and soil moisture, the land acted as a furnace, according to the National Oceanic and Atmospheric Assoc. "The climate of that region took on desert qualities, accentuating its capacity to produce heat," NOAA summarizes on its website.

In July 1936, a record heat wave swept across Minnesota, bringing with it the highest temperature ever recorded in the state—114 degrees in Moorhead on July 6, 1936, tying a record set in Beardsley in 1917. Pipestone logged 15 straight days of 100 degrees or more. Duluth had two 100-degree days. According to the *Minnesota Weather Almanac*, "At Beardsley, in Big Stone County, 13 consecutive July days brought temperatures of 100 degrees or higher. That same heat spell produced five such consecutive days in the Twin Cities, inspiring many citizens to sleep on porches, in backyards, or in city parks."

Nationally, about 5,000 deaths were associated with the 1936 heat wave.

That was the worst of the worst. But trouble was far from over. According to a 1988 *Star Tribune* story: "In 1937, Minnesota Gov. Elmer A. Benson sent a telegram to Harry Hopkins, who ran the federal Works Progress Administration:

MANY FARMERS IN DROUGHT STRICKEN COUNTIES OF MINNESOTA IN FINANCIAL DISTRESS STOP RESETTLEMENT GRANTS WHOLLY INADEQUATE FOR SUBSISTENCE NEEDS LET ALONE LIVESTOCK

*FEED AND SEED STOP PLEASE DO EVERYTHING
POSSIBLE TO EMPLOY THE MOST NEEDY ON WPA
THEREBY INCREASING THEIR MONTHLY AID TO
TIDE THEM OVER UNTIL NEXT HARVEST."*

In 1937, Minnesota added 10 new state parks, thanks
to the Works Progress Administration. It began to rain in 1938
and 1939. By 1941, most areas of the country were receiving
near-normal rainfalls. The rain, along with the outbreak of
World War II, alleviated many of the hardships of the 1930s. In
fact, new production demands brought the United States into
a rapid economic boom.

The legacy of the Dust Bowl lives on in modern
conservation and farming practices, and in the art, music
and literature of the time. While the Dust Bowl yielded
sparse crops, it did produce a crop of artists whose work will
forever tell the story of this unrelenting decade. Created as
part of the New Deal, the Farm Security Administration hired
photographers such as Walker Evans, Dorothea Lange and
Gordon Parks to document the plight of the poor farmer. The
FSA also funded two documentary films by Pare Lorentz, *The
Plow That Broke the Plains* about the Dust Bowl and *The River*
about the Mississippi River.

John Steinbeck's Nobel- and Pulitzer Prize-winning
novel, *The Grapes of Wrath*, set during the Dust Bowl, was
published in 1939. The following year, John Ford directed the
movie of the same name, starring Henry Fonda.

Folk singer Woody Guthrie came to public attention
with his first recording, the *Dust Bowl Ballads*, songs he penned

and performed throughout the 1930s and released in 1940. In his liner notes, Guthrie wrote: "This bunch of songs are 'Oakie' songs, 'Dust Bowl' songs, 'Migracious' songs, about my folks and my relatives, about a jillion of 'em, that got hit by the drought, the dust, the wind, the banker, and the landlord, and the police, all at the same time. ..."

Guthrie chronicled the era on songs like "Dusty Old Dust (So Long, It's Been Good to Know Yuh)," setting the stage for future balladeers to do the same in their time:

The churches was jammed and the churches was packed
An' that dusty old dust storm blowed so black
Preacher could not read a word of his text
An' he folded his specs, an' took up collection, sayin'

So long, it's been good to know yuh
So long, it's been good to know yuh
So long, it's been good to know yuh
This dusty old dust is a gettin' my home
And I got to be driftin' along

Farm abandoned after successive years of drought, possibly near Breckenridge.
(photo: Minnesota Historical Society)

View during drought of the St. Croix River, at Mueller's Boat Livery, Stillwater.
(photo: Minnesota Historical Society)

Members of the Holden Congregation of the Norwegian Lutheran Church, praying for a break in the drought, south of Beardsley. (photo: Minnesota Historical Society)

Drought farmers working on farm in Foster township, south of Beardsley.
(photo: Minnesota Historical Society)

President Franklin D. Roosevelt's drought conference in Des Moines, Iowa.
(photo: Minnesota Historical Society)

Dust bowl scene, Swift County. (photo: Minnesota Historical Society)

Six twisters tore across the Twin Cities May 6, 1965, including two tornadoes in Fridley.
(photo: courtesy *Star Tribune*)

The 1965 Tornadoes
'The Greatest Weather Disaster in Twin Cities History'

In spring 1965, The Minnesota Twins were on their way to building a winning season that would put them in their first World Series at the Metropolitan Stadium. With stars like Mudcat Grant and Al Worthington on the mound (raking in the team's highest salaries at $21,500 and $22,000, respectively), and other legends like Harmon Killebrew and Tony Oliva on the roster—it was a storybook year for Minnesota baseball, one that Minnesotans would nostalgically re-live for decades.

But it was a heartwrenching story that year for Minnesotans affected by weather, with two 1965 storms tying for fifth place in the Minnesota State Climatology Office's list of the Most Significant Minnesota Weather Events of the 20th Century: the Mississippi and Minnesota River flooding, and the May 5-6 tornado outbreak. (See the first book in The Minnesota Series, *Storms!*, for an account of the 1965 flooding.)

Less than a month after rivers in southern Minnesota and the Twin Cities overflowed their banks and ultimately claimed 15 lives, and mere days after President Lyndon Johnson declared the Minnesota regions disaster areas and released $3 million in aid—devastating weather struck again. On May 6, 1965, the Twins were home for the last night of a three-night stand against the Baltimore Orioles when historic tornadoes blew into town. According to the State Climatology

Office: "Six twisters touched down in or close to the metro area. Particularly hard hit was Fridley, with two of the tornadoes crossing the city. In all, 13 people died due to the storms. The event has been called the greatest weather disaster in Twin Cities history."

A precurser came the day before in southcentral Minnesota, when eight tornadoes struck, including three that were rated F4 (indicating winds 207-260 mph). There, 11 people were killed and 81 were injured. The next day, the most damaging series of tornadoes in Minnesota invaded the western and northern sections of the Twin Cities between 6 and 9 p.m. In addition to the 13 Twin Cities deaths, 685 were injured, and damage was estimated in excess of 50 million dollars, according to the National Weather Service.

Warnings from the U.S. Weather Bureau and diligent reporting by media, in particular WCCO Radio, are credited with averting further deaths. Poor communications during the "Palm Sunday tornado outbreak" the month before, on April 11, taught weather watchers across the country a lesson in preparedness. On that day, 51 tornadoes tore through the Great Lakes region, killing 256 people in six states. During the April outbreaks, the U.S. Weather Bureau warned of approaching severe weather. But power outages and limited communications systems cut off many residents in Midwestern states.

By the time the May tornadoes rolled in, Minnesota cities for the first time used civil defense sirens to warn of severe weather. A notable exception: Fridley did not have a siren. One out of every four homes in Fridley was destroyed by the 1965 tornadoes. (Initially designed to warn of air raids in World War II, outdoor civil defense sirens were adapted to warn of nuclear attack during the cold war. They were adapted yet again to warn against natural disasters such as tornadoes and floods and are still in use for that purpose.)

The website www.radiotapes.com has a recording of WCCO Radio's May 6 Twin Cities tornado broadcasts (which would earn WCCO a Peabody Award for informing citizens of the danger). WCCO's first warning to the public came at the end of the 5:35 to 6 p.m. Howard Viken program. Thirty minutes later, Dick Chapman was on duty, announcing the night's first tornado warning. Through the next three hours, Chapman and Charlie Boone intermingled Weather Bureau warnings with live reports from eyewitnesses, who called from their basements in Excelsior, Chanhassen, Brooklyn Center, Fridley, Hopkins and Minneapolis, reporting funnels in progress, and of houses destroyed, roofs flying.

At 7:25 p.m., listener Robert Clark from Fridley called in, reporting he had been in his car when the tornado came, blowing in his car windows. He described a funnel touching down at Fridley Jr. High School, which tore the roof off the gymnasium and blew in the east side of the building. "But no one was hurt. None of the children assembled for the spring carnival was injured," he said. "All the children were laying down on the floor in the building, and no one was injured."

Tragically, Clark, who called with these reports of survival, was believed to have been among those killed by a second Fridley tornado later that evening.

According to the National Weather Service Weather Forecast Office, the sequence of events was:

Tornado No. 1 touched down at 6:08 p.m. just east of Cologne in Carver County, was on the ground for 13 miles, and dissipated in the northwestern portion of Minnetrista in Hennepin County. It was rated an F4, killed three people and injured 175.

Tornado 2 touched down at 6:27 p.m. near Lake Susan in Chanhassen and traveled seven miles straight north to Deephaven. It was rated an F4, but resulted in no injuries or fatalities.

Tornado 3 touched down at 6:34 p.m. about three miles east of New Auburn in Sibley County and moved to just west of Lester Prairie in McLeod County. On the ground for 16 miles, it was rated an F3, but there were no injuries or fatalities.

Tornado 4 touched down at 6:43 p.m. about two miles east of Green Isle in Sibley County, was on the ground for 11 miles, and dissipated about two miles southwest of Waconia. It was rated an F2, killed one person, and injured 175.

Tornado 5 touched down at 7:06 p.m. in the southwesternmost corner of Fridley, moved across the Northern Ordnance plant, and dissipated just northeast of Laddie Lake in Blaine. It was on the ground for seven miles, reached F4 intensity, killed three people and injured 175.

Tornado 6 touched down at 8:14 p.m. in Golden Valley, moved across north Minneapolis and into Fridley, then Mounds View, and finally dissipated just west of Centerville. This was rated a force F4, killed six people and injured 158, and was on the ground for 18 miles.

While storms raged in 11 counties the evening of May
6, oddly, the Minnesota Twins were able to play that night at
The Met in Bloomington, outdoors. They lost, 1-5 against the
Orioles, after winning the two previous nights. But things would
look up again. They were on their way to a pennant victory,
and as Twin Citians rebuilt from the devastating tornadoes,
they made time to cheer on their Twins. According to baseball-
almanac.com, some 1.46 million fans witnessed the 1965 Twins
finish the season with a .630 winning percentage.

U.S. Weather Bureau agents on the scene to survey the Fridley damage.
(photo: courtesy of NOAA/National Weather Service Twin Cities)

Mounds View was hit hard by the tornadoes. (photo: courtesy of NOAA/National
Weather Service Twin Cities)

Twin Cities cars and homes were toppled on May 6, 1965. (photo: courtesy of NOAA/ National Weather Service Twin Cities)

Suburban homes and outlying farms were devastated by the tornadoes. (photo: courtesy of NOAA/National Weather Service Twin Cities)

In this house east of Hamburg and southeast of Norwood, five people were in the basement when a tornado struck; none were injured. (photo: courtesy of NOAA/ National Weather Service Twin Cities)

Homes were crumbled across Fridley after two tornadoes tore through the city May 6, 1965. (photo: courtesy of NOAA/National Weather Service Twin Cities)

U.S. Weather Bureau personnel examined the damage in Fridley after the 1965 tornadoes.
(photo: courtesy of NOAA/National Weather Service Twin Cities)

Mobile homes in Fridley were turned over in the twister.
(photo: courtesy of NOAA/National Weather Service Twin Cities)

The Superbowl Blizzard defeated this banner in Minneapolis much like the Pittsburgh Steelers defeated the Vikings. This photo is from the cover of the Jan. 13, 1975 *St. Paul Dispatch*. (photo: Minnesota Historical Society)

The 1975 Blizzard of the Century
Snowy Road En Route to a Vikings Super Bowl

Merrily clashing with the traditional reds and greens of the holiday season of 1974 in Minnesota was a vibrant shade of purple. On Dec. 29, 1974, the Minnesota Vikings defeated the LA Rams at The Met, and the buzz around the state as the new year dawned was that the "Purple People Eaters" were heading to their second Super Bowl, this time against Pittsburgh's "Steel Curtain," on Jan. 12, 1975.

But every good Vikings fan knows the road to a Vikings Super Bowl is never easy, and before Minnesotans could hunker down in front of their black-and-white TV sets to watch Terry Bradshaw and Fran Tarkenton do battle in New Orleans, they would first be shoveling snow—a *lot* of it.

The "Storm of the Century" (as meteorologists dubbed it) hit Minnesota Jan. 10-12, 1975, arriving on the anniversary of Minnesota's worst blizzard ever on record—the tragic Children's Blizzard, which claimed 200 lives in Minnesota, and 500 in the Upper Midwest.

The '75 storm (also called The Great Storm of 1975, the Super Bowl Blizzard and, elsewhere across the country, the Tornado Outbreak of January 1975) would remain the worst winter storm in Minnesota in modern times until 1991, when the Halloween Blizzard that year changed the record books again.

The storm was an intense system that impacted a large portion of the central and southeastern United States from

Jan. 9 to 12. According to Wikipedia: "The storm produced 45 tornadoes in the southeast United States, resulting in 12 fatalities, while later dropping over two feet of snow and killing 58 people in the Midwest."

In Minnesota, 35 people died as a result of the '75 storm—14 from the blizzard and 21 from related heart attacks.

Beginning in the Pacific Ocean, the storm hit the Northwest Pacific coast with gale force winds on Jan. 8. "At the same time," says Wikipedia, "Arctic air was being drawn southward from Canada into the Great Plains, and large amounts of warm tropical air from the Gulf of Mexico were being pulled northward into much of the eastern U.S. The storm moved from Colorado into Oklahoma before turning northward toward the Upper Midwest. ... As the storm system began to move northeastward out of Oklahoma, the cool air pulled down behind the system interacted with the moisture being pulled northward to produce snow over a large part of the Midwest."

By Jan. 10, the snow began to fall—as much as 23.5 inches at International Falls—and temperatures began to drop. Duluth's high temperatures fell from 33 degrees on Jan. 11 to -3 degrees on Jan. 12. For three days, Minnesotans faced all of winter's wrath— snow, rain, sleet, freezing rain, falling temperatures and more. Record-setting low-pressure readings were recorded in Rochester (28.63 inches), the Twin Cities (28.62 inches) and Duluth (28.55 inches). Winds gusted 50 to 80 mph, creating snowdrifts 20 feet high, and roads were closed in the state, some for 11 days. In Willmar, 168 passengers were stranded in a train for hours, unable to walk to shelter because of dangerously low wind chill.

Throughout the upper Midwest, thousands of motorists were stranded. Just east of Sioux Falls, a 2,000-foot broadcast tower collapsed. Livestock losses were estimated at more than 100,000—including 15,000 cattle, 15,000 hogs, 1,500 sheep and 70,000 chickens. The governor of Iowa requested that 40 northwest counties be declared disaster areas.

Across the country, weather records were set during this storm. It remains one of the worst blizzards ever to strike parts of the Midwest, as well as one of the largest January tornado outbreaks on record in the United States.

1975 continued to be a tough year for Minnesota weather. Another blizzard struck March 23-25 across southwestern and central Minnesota, with heavy snows and gusting winds. Many roads were blocked by drifts up to 20 feet, including I-35, from Forest Lake to Duluth. According to the National Weather Service, "a foot of snow and winds unofficially recorded in excess of 100 mph paralyzed the city of Duluth. Waves up to 20 feet pounded the Lake Superior shore, flooding basements and blowing out store windows. Waves and ice buckled a metal and glass safety wall at a lakefront motel, forcing evacuation of 10 rooms as knee-deep water flooded into hallways. Waves destroyed a 40-foot wall at Two Harbors, flooding municipal water pumping stations. Large chunks of beach along Lake Superior shore were washed away."

With little time to rest, yet another blizzard came to Minnesota March 26-29, bringing snow of 4 to 17 inches. In Duluth, the airport, businesses and schools were closed.

The most infamous weather event of the year—immortalized in song and story—came Nov. 10, 1975, when a storm sank the Edmund Fitzgerald in Lake Superior, killing all 29 crew members.

The Vikings lost to Pittsburgh in that real-life Super Bowl Blizzard of 1975. But Minnesota fans can take some consolation in "winning" the night before. On Jan. 11, Super Bowl eve, *The Mary Tyler Moore Show* (set in a fictitious television newsroom in Minneapolis) used this game as the story line.

According to Wikipedia: "Lou Grant was teaching Ted Baxter how to bet on football games, and used Ted's money, as well as some of his own to bet on the Vikings winning the Super Bowl. The Vikings won the Super Bowl in this episode but Ted's hopes were dashed when it was revealed that Lou actually bet all the money on the Steelers. At the end of the show, Mary Tyler Moore announced the following over the credits: 'If the Pittsburgh Steelers win the actual Super Bowl tomorrow, we want to apologize to the Pittsburgh team and their fans for this purely fictional story. If on the other hand, they lose, remember, you heard it here first.' "

THE BRAINERD DAILY DISPATCH

"CENTRAL MINNESOTA'S DAILY NEWSPAPER"

In the Heart of the Lake Region | Member of The Associated Press | United Press International Telephoto Service | BRAINERD, MINNESOTA, 56401, SATURDAY, JANUARY 11, 1975 | SINGLE COPY 15 CENTS | VOL. 99B—NO. 134

Blizzard Buries Brainerd, State

Brainerd began to dig itself out today from under one of the worst blizzards to hit here since Armistice Day, 1940, with unofficial estimates recording 14 to 16 inches of new snow.

(With today's edition to The Brainerd Daily Dispatch, this newspaper has not missed publishing a paper for at least 43 years, including the Armistice Day storm.)

Drifting snow closed off most downtown streets to car travel, with most stores in the central business district and at the Mall reported closed for the day.

District maintenance offices of the State Highway Patrol recommended no travel any where in the state until the winds subside.

Unofficial reports put the temperature here at presstime at 9 below, with winds blowing at 30 to 40 miles per hour and gusting to 60 miles per hour. An estimated 10 inches of snow was reported at midnight last night.

Leo Dechaine, a dispatcher at the Crow Wing Cooperative Power and Light Company, reported scattered power outages in the Brainerd area, in Mission Township, Lastrup, Miller Lake and the south side of Horseshoe Lake.

"We're working with the county now," he said. "The county is plowing out ahead of us. We can't get all the trucks out."

Dechaine reported about 30 calls during the night, most from area residents concerned about possible electrical outages.

The heavy snowfall closed the Brainerd Airport, and shut off air traffic into the county.

Brainerd Police reported no serious emergencies in the city. They are presently using a four-wheel drive vehicle for emergencies only.

Policemen reported a number of calls offering assistance in the event of an emergency situation.

Terry Moberg of the Brainerd Ambulance Service, reported three runs last night and one today, using his special emergency rescue sled, a snowmobile equipped with an enclosed trailer.

At 11:30 last night, 1½-year-old Melissa Monson of Baxter was brought in to St. Joseph's Hospital after suffering a seizure. She is reported in good condition today.

A second run at 2:30 a.m. was made to the Russel Jordan home, 1704 Oak Street. Jordan, 51, reported abdominal pains. He also is reported in good condition at St. Joseph's Hospital.

A woman undergoing labor pains was brought to St. Joseph's at 6 a.m., Moberg said. She arrived safely and is under observation.

Moberg took the ambulance out this forenoon to bring in a second expectant mother from rural Brainerd. Snowplows preceded the ambulance all the way in and out, he said.

City snowplow crews were pulled off early this morning due to high winds which caused drifting conditions, according to George Kriha, city engineer.

Kriha said the plows will not go back out until later tonight or when the winds die down.

No north-south or east-west plowing time schedules have been established yet. The plows will travel down the main streets as their first priority, he said.

The National Weather Service issued winter storm warnings for today and tonight, with blizzard conditions, heavy and blowing snow, for both today and tonight.

The high temperature in the state was in the low teens, dropping to 10 to 15 below this afternoon.

The low tonight was predicted at 20 to 30 below, with diminishing winds and snows.

By The Associated Press

A paralyzing blizzard smashed into Minnesota, leaving hundreds stranded in towns and cities and on farms behind drifted roads including some 300 travelers at the St. Cloud Civic Center.

The State Highway Department advised today against travel until winds subside and plowing crews can get out.

Many highways had a slick surface under the snow from Friday's slushy downpour that preceded the blizzard and plunging temperatures.

At St. Cloud, in the central part of the state, a reporter estimated 300 were housed in the Civic Center. About half of them were passengers came from the Greyhound bus depot half a block away. At least six buses had to pull off highways at St. Cloud.

Civil Defense and Red Cross personnel helped care for those stranded. Al Baert, regional civil defense officer, said, "It's horrible in the central part of the state."

He advised any persons having to make emergency trips to call law enforcement agencies for help.

Two persons at the Civic Center suffered mild coronaries, said Baert. One was taken to a hospital.

Snow that began piling up Friday and continued today measured over 12 inches in some areas, and drifted several feet.

At Fairmont, near the Iowa border, drifts piled as high as 10 feet, workers at the municipal water plant reported.

Two pregnant women were brought to a Fairmont hospital, but only after several rescue vehicles were used. When three smaller ones got stuck, a heavy construction machine broke through drifts.

The Blizzard Snowmobile Club had brought a doctor to one of the women's homes.

Fairmont was at a standstill and police barricaded roads out of town.

One farmer in the area called the Martin County sheriff's office to report a transformer burning on a utility pole 50 feet from his barn.

"Just watch it burn, we can't get to you," the officer advised.

Another farmer who went out by snowmobile late Friday to check his cattle didn't make it back. He wisely took refuge in a culvert and got home this morning, authorities said.

The Fairmont Sentinel didn't go to press when workers couldn't get to the office.

Other sections of southern Minnesota were immobilized.

In Brown County, all roads were closed.

A woman snowmobiler was reported missing in Nicollet County. Fellow snowmobilers searched Friday night but quit at 3 a.m. because of poor visibility and snow.

Another missing person report came from Faribault County, where someone went to help a neighbor at 1:30 a.m.

Electric power was out at several places, when icing snapped lines. Among them were Faribault, Sibley County and near LeCenter. Some householders without power to operate furnaces took refuge with neighbors.

Five persons were stranded in a car near a trailer court at North Mankato.

The Mower County sheriff's office said five cars were stranded north of Brownsdale, Minn. A highway cruiser checking cars found all were empty.

Although Minneapolis-St. Paul hadn't got the full brunt of the storm by this morning, activity was crippled.

Greyhound and other commercial buses remained at garages. A maintenance worker for Greyhound estimated 60 buses were halted at Minneapolis. He said all Greyhound buses in the area had gotten to towns and he knew of none stalled on highways.

At the Minneapolis-St. Paul International Airport, the tower said flights were down some 50 per cent.

Several Twin Cities stores closed for the day.

The National Weather Service said the snow would continue heavy in Minnesota throughout Saturday night.

It was the first vicious taste of winter for most Minnesotans, who hadn't even had below-zero temperatures in many sections

STORM
Continued on Page 2

A LOST CAUSE—Snow removal equipment was out this morning in what had to be a losing battle against the elements as a ferocious storm struck Brainerd and much of the Upper Midwest last night and today. The city pulled off its plows shortly after this picture was taken and City Engineer George Kriha says plowing will not resume until the wind dies down. (Dispatch Photo)

AFTERMATH — A Shopping Center in McComb, Miss. was completely destroyed yesterday by a tornado which also leveled homes and damaged schools in the city. There are numerous reported deaths in the area and many injured. (UPI Telephoto)

Tornadoes Blitz South

MCCOMB, Miss. (AP) — A series of deadly tornadoes that swooped down out of a fast-moving storm in Dixie have left at least 11 persons known dead, some 200 injured and patches of destruction in four states.

A 12th person was reported missing, and officials estimated damage in the millions.

The wonder of it was that more were not killed by the swirling winds which struck Friday.

For instance, a twister smashed into an elementary school here while 300 pupils crouched in the hallways, but the most serious injury was a broken leg.

Another tornado ripped the roof from a school gym in Opelousas, La., while 600 youngsters cowered on the floor. The only injuries were a few bruises.

"We may have seen a miracle that more people weren't killed," said Mississippi Gov. Bill Waller as he inspected damage here and moved to have McComb declared a disaster area.

McComb, a southwest Mississippi city of 39,900, was hardest hit of a dozen towns that suffered tornado damage. It had four dead and 115 injured. Mayor John Thompson said 300 homes were ruined, leaving 750 in emergency shelter.

Three more were killed in the nearby town of Ruth, and two died on U.S. 90 near Pascagoula when a tractor-trailer was whipped sideways and two cars smashed into it.

At Lake Charles, 20-year-old Ronnie Benoit of Jennings died in a hospital early today of injuries received when a twister hit Mermentau.

A crewman was missing and presumed drowned when a tugboat capsized on Lake Pontchartrain near New Orleans.

At Ragland, Ala., a man died when a twister ripped up a service station shortly after another tornado had smashed some 100 houses, 75 mobile homes and 25 stores in nearby Pell City.

Alabama Civil Defense Director C.J. Sullivan estimated that 50 persons were injured at Pell City and 12 at Ragland. He also said a twister was reported at Pelham south of Birmingham. High winds were reported at Lahett.

Near Fort Walton Beach, Fla., about 20 mobile homes were heavily damaged by another tornado, but no serious injuries were reported.

National Guardsmen patroled in McComb and Pell City today to prevent looting.

The tornadoes were spawned by a squall line which developed near the Louisiana-Texas border Friday morning and then moved rapidly eastward

TORNADO
Continued on Page 2

Hasskamp Resigns

Ken Hasskamp has announced his resignation from the office of District Court Commissioner.

Hasskamp, a 20-year-old university student from Crosby, was sworn in last Monday. On Tuesday, the county board of commissioners here asked for a legal opinion on whether Hasskamp met the age requirements for public office.

State law requires public office holders to be 21 or older.

In a letter to the county board, Hasskamp said that he is voluntarily resigning the post.

"After examining the Minnesota Constitution and other sources of legal information," he wrote, "it seems obvious that the age requirement for all public office holders in the state is 21, not 18 as I believed."

"Since I have not attained that legal age I will, therefore, resign the office of Crow Wing County Court Commissioner, effective immediately."

Hasskamp noted that he was submitting his resignation "reluctantly."

"I would very much like to challenge the 21-year-old state requirement, but I have neither the time nor the financial resources necessary to pursue the question further," he wrote.

Hasskamp was elected Nov. 5 by three write-in votes, tieing for the post with Don O'Brien, county board member. O'Brien stepped out of the race, since he would have to give up his county board post to take the court commissioner position.

State law now allows the district court here to appoint a county resident to the post.

Weather

MINNESOTA: Near blizzard conditions through and early tonight over northeast portion. Blowing and drifting snow with occasional light snow or flurries with strong gusty surface winds and quite cold temperatures will cause near blizzard conditions over state the rest of today and northeast protion early tonight. Light snow or flurries and quite cold tonight and Sunday. Lows tonight 17 below to 17 below. Highs Sunday 12 below

LOCAL WEATHER

Since Walter Wieland Field was closed today due to the storm, The Dispatch was unable to obtain the local temperature readings.

Fred Harris To Run For Presidency

CONCORD, N.H. (AP) — Former Sen. Fred R. Harris of Oklahoma announced his candidacy today for the 1976 Democratic presidential nomination, calling for an attack on forces preventing "full employment and fair taxes."

Harris, 44, told a news conference he would run "a people's campaign — both in strategy and in beliefs."

Harris, who calls himself a "new populist," stressed economic problems as the central theme of his campaign.

HE DOESN'T MIND — Shep, Dispatch photographer Ron Canfield's dog, seems to be enjoying the snow which struck here beginning yesterday. No official figures were available on the amount of snow, but estimates placed it at 12-14 inches.

School Board Committee Airs Rental Fees, Audit

The Brainerd School Board's finance committee met for a brief session yesterday, discussing rental fees for school facilities and the upcoming school audit.

The committee met at noon Friday, in the high school board room.

Members reviewed the school district's policy and fees for rental of school facilities, and recommended that they remain the same as those presently in force.

The school's policy at present is to allow use of school facilities by non-profit groups at no charge, with the exception of custodial fees.

If the activity is held during hours when a custodian is on duty, there is no charge.

These groups include such organizations as the Lake Area Music group, Campfire and Boy Scout groups, and local PTA's.

Other groups or individuals are charged hourly or daily rates for use of school facilities.

The rate schedule is presently as follows: individual rooms, $4 per hour; Franklin and Washington Junior High School auditoriums, $35 per day; Franklin gym, $35 per day; Washington gym, $50; Franklin and Washington cafeterias, $50 per day; elementary school auditoriums, $25; senior high school cafeterias, $100 per day; senior high pool, $20 per hour plus life guard fees, and elementary school auditoriums, $25 per day.

These charges do not include additional fees for custodial services.

All rentals are arranged through the building principal. Special rates have been allowed for groups using facilities for two or three days.

The second subject under discussion Friday concerned a request by a local auditing firm to do the yearly school audit, in place of the public examiner's office.

The committee supported the recomendation of Eugene McKee, district business manager, to stay with the state examiner.

The original request to change school policy came from Darrel Johns, a local C.P.A., who met with the board last November.

Johns asked to have the school audit opened to competitive bidding among local auditing firms. The audit this year is scheduled for June. The cost last year, using the public examiner's office, was about $5,200.

McKee recommended, however, that the school use the

SCHOOL
Continued on Page 2

Brainerd was paralyzed by the '75 blizzard.

The corner of Seventh and Hennepin in downtown Minneapolis was nearly deserted at noon on Jan. 11, 1975. (photo: Minnesota Historical Society)

Jumper cables helped start cars in the bitter cold on Jan. 11, 1975 in downtown
Minneapolis. (photo: Minnesota Historical Society)

While the blizzard of 1975 grounded Minnesotans, Bud Grant, Fran Tarkenton and
The Vikings prepared to take on the Steelers in sunny New Orleans' Tulane Stadium.
(photo: Minnesota Historical Society)

Snow drifted under bridges near Albert Lea.
(photo: Minnesota Historical Society)

In Faribault, I35 was closed due to snow, cold and wind.
(photo: Minnesota Historical Society)

The 1981 tornado bears down on Minneapolis.
(photo: Minnesota Historical Society)

The 1981 Edina/Roseville Tornado
Twister in the City ... Again

Suddenly the wind burst powerfully through the open windows. ... The curtains blew almost parallel to the floor briefly. Then, just as quickly as the wind started, it reversed and sucked outward, drawing the curtains out to the screens.

–Notes from Minneapolis website about the June 14, 1981 tornado

Old Glory was getting a workout in Minnesota June 14, 1981, flags flapping furiously in violent winds at patriotic homes and buildings across the Twin Cities. It was Flag Day that summer Sunday when a force F3 tornado ripped across the metro area, killing one man in its 15-mile path from Edina to Roseville.

A National Weather Service summary puts to rest years of this storm's name confusion with its statement about the event: "Folks on the east side of the Twin Cities call it the 'Har Mar Tornado' while others west of the Mississippi tend to prefer 'Lake Harriet' or 'Edina Tornado.' No matter the name, it was the most significant tornado to hit the Twin Cities since the 1965 Fridley-Mounds View tornadoes."

Meteorologist Jonathan Yuhas recalls the storm on his KARE-11 blog: "The day started warm and humid in the Twin Cities with sunshine and temperatures quickly climbing into the low-80s by the noon hour. The supercell thunderstorm that produced the tornado first brought large hail to Eden Prairie in the mid-afternoon, then a tornado developed over Edina and was difficult to see because it was wrapped in heavy rain. The tornado first hit the northeastern part of Edina around Arden Park and then moved into the 50th and France area. The tornado then moved northeast into south Minneapolis around Lake Harriet and as it moved northeast toward Roseville it continued to get bigger and stronger."

According to the official record, a tornado watch was posted at 3 p.m. At 3:49, a tornado touched down in Edina about one-third mile southwest of the intersection of 50th and France. The tornado traveled across Lake Harriet, and the National Weather Service issued a tornado warning and the area-wide siren activation at 3:53. This activated 200 sirens in eastern Hennepin, Ramsey, and small portions of Anoka and Dakota counties.

A Minneapolis meditation group was finding little serenity in their meeting in a south Minneapolis home that day. According to the group's website, recalling the June tornado: "The sky was overcast and rainy and the temperatures were warm, so we had the windows open to let air in the chapel. … Despite my best efforts at concentrating within, I could nevertheless hear the thunder and lightening increase in intensity to the point where it sounded like constant thunder. … Suddenly the wind burst powerfully through the open windows, blowing papers from our information table in the back of the chapel onto the floor. The curtains blew almost parallel to the floor briefly. Then, just as quickly as the wind started, it reversed and sucked outward, drawing the curtains out to the screens."

Organizers of the Edina Art Fair on 50th and France were no doubt grateful they had wrapped up the week before.

The meditation group recalled that, after their meeting, they "walked up to 50th and France Avenue, about three blocks away, and noticed the Edina Theater marquee tumbled onto the street, trees downed, and a florist shop's windows shattered. Indeed, we had had a close call with a tornado, which after coming through our neighborhood had headed northeast, passed over Lake Harriet and continued over Interstate Highway 35W beyond."

The National Weather Service reports the tornado's path length was continuous for 15 miles over a 26-minute period, varying from 75 yards to two-and-a-half city blocks. Wind speeds varied from 80 mph in the narrow width areas to as high as 160 mph in the wider path areas. In all, 83 people were injured and one person was killed: 20-year-old Allen Wheeler was fishing along the shore of Lake Harriet when a tree fell on him. Total damages from the storm were estimated at $47 million, according to *Minnesota Weather Almanac.*

The Har Mar Mall area was hit hard, with businesses and homes destroyed. The Red Cross set up temporary shelters in Roseville and Minneapolis, and some 120 National Guardsmen were activated in Roseville to prevent looting of damaged homes and businesses. "The largest problem was from the throngs of sightseers who drove to view the damage and caused quite a hindrance to clean-up activity," said the National Weather Service. "One homeowner posted a sign: 'The residents bitterly resent your morbid curiosity. Why don't you stop gawking and go home.' "

One business turned their losses into long-term business gain. After the tornado leveled the Sound of

Music Roseville store, and the store was forced to liquidate quickly—the company responded with a "Tornado Sale," slashing prices and selling products in the ruins of the store. It was an astounding success, a turning point for the struggling company—and the concept of low prices in a "no-frills environment" was born. The results of that promotion prompted company founder Richard Schulze to open a chain of superstores under the name Best Buy.

"The overwhelming response to lower prices led Schulze to introduce low audio and video prices in a 'no-frills' retail environment," according to www.historyofamericanbusiness.com. "Again, adaptation had paid off. Later that year Best Buy added photography and home office products. The result was a model of retail efficiency. The stores averaged $350 in sales per square foot compared to the industry averages of $150–$200 per square foot."

There was comparatively little warning that day when the tornado ripped into the Twin Cities. Since Doppler radar (which records wind speeds and identifies areas of rotation within thunderstorms) has been in use, the warning time for tornadoes has grown from an average of five minutes in the 1980s to an average of 13 minutes today, according to *National Geographic*. But in 1981, The National Weather Service in Chanhassen still used conventional radar. The more precise Doppler radar was just beginning to be used for weather surveillance.

If the same conditions were to occur today, sirens would be sounded earlier. "I don't think 19 minutes of lead time would have been unthinkable," said Rich Naistat, science operations officer with the Chanhassen office of the National Weather Service (NWS) in a *Star Tribune* story.

The Chanhassen office installed Doppler in the '90s. The addition of more NWS radio transmitters and a close relationship with media outlets also has aided in spotting tornadoes. "An energetic spotter network has been the key to alerting the public in Minnesota," according to NWS. "In fact, the increasing number of tornadoes reported may be a direct result of improved communications networks, public awareness, warning systems and training."

The Edina Theater marquee fell victim to the tornado that swept from 50th and France to Roseville. (photo: Minnesota Historical Society)

This Chevette near Pleasant Avenue South in Minneapolis was no match for trees brought down by the storm. (photo: Minnesota Historical Society)

Trees in south Minneapolis littered the streets.
(photo: Minnesota Historical Society)

In Roseville, near Har Mar Mall, Color Tile and Sound of Music (later to become Best Buy Stores) were destroyed by the winds. (photos: Minnesota Historical Society)

Twisted trees across the Twin Cities showed the effects of the turbulence.
(photo: Minnesota Historical Society)

The 1997 Red River Valley Flooding
'Come Hell and High Water'

The apocalypse came with ice and fire. I was among the many journalists who covered the disaster and I will never forget the sensation of standing in freezing water in hip boots while ashes fell on my head from the sky. All we needed was Charlton Heston to send Egyptian chariots into the water and I would've sworn we were all extras in a remake of The Ten Commandments.

–Nick Coleman, *Star Tribune* 2007, recalling the
1997 flooding in Grand Forks

The warnings came early the winter of 1996-'97: Come spring, there would be flooding in the Red River Valley. Of that, there was no doubt. It was a familiar seasonal refrain to the people who had learned to live on one of the flattest expanses of land on earth, which 10,000 years ago formed the floor of glacial Lake Agassiz. But this time, the warning would yield life-changing results. Soon, residents would experience the most severe flooding of the Red River since 1826.

By May, the 1997 flood would devastate the cities of Grand Forks, N.D., and East Grand Forks, Minn.—forcing 60,000 residents there to evacuate and 80,000 people total in river towns in Minnesota, North Dakota and Canada. Eleven people in three states would be killed.

The Red flows north (the result of how the glacier melted), emptying into Lake Winnipeg in Canada. Along the way, it forms the boundary between North Dakota and Minne-

Tony Wamback pulls his son, Nick, 3, down Main Street April 13, 1997, in Georgetown, Minn. (photo: AP/The Forum, Andy Blenkush)

sota, beginning at Wahpeton, N.D.-Breckenridge, Minn., continuing north to Fargo-Moorhead, then Grand Forks-East Grand Forks, and on to Canada. The northerly flow makes the Red prone to flooding. Snow and ice in the southern portion of the river melt first. Yet, colder temperatures farther north (downstream) keep the river largely frozen. This may cause ice jams to form, and substantial backup can occur.

The flatness of the Red's lake plain (not really a "river valley" at all) enhances flooding, since there is very little slope for rain or melting snow. "When a North Dakota river overflows its banks, there is no topography to constrain flood waters, which may spread out over a very wide area, increasing damage," according to www.riverwatchonline, Prairie Public Television's information site about the Red River. It's like pouring water on a tabletop—there is nowhere for the overflowing river to go but to stretch out into a massive lake, for miles.

In addition, the sediment of the area, left behind by the retreating glacier, makes for some of the richest soil and best farmland in the world—but it is relatively impermeable to water. As a result, water ponds up and flows into the rivers and streams, adding to flood levels.

All of these elements were in play the winter of 1996-'97.

It all started with a rainy fall, and the ground became saturated. Then came one of the harshest winters in memory, dumping record snowfall on the Valley. Blizzards began in November and continued through spring—eight of them, bringing a record 117 inches of snow to Fargo and 98.6 inches to Grand Forks. On Jan. 11, the North Dakota National Guard was activated to clear snow from roadways, and President Bill Clinton declared North Dakota, South Dakota and Minnesota federal disaster areas. On Jan. 14-16, Minnesota Gov. Arne Carlson closed all Minnesota schools.

Besides the record snowfall, record low temperatures came to the upper Midwest that winter. Between Nov. 7, 1996 and March 18, 1997 (a span of 131 days), the air temperature reached 40 degrees only three times in Grand Forks, according to Wikipedia. Because there were only a few days above freezing, there was little gradual melting of snow. Then, starting on March 19, the temperature rose above freezing for 27 consecutive days. The sudden warmth melted the snow too quickly for the river to handle.

More records were about to be broken. On Feb. 28, the National Weather Service announced that spring melting could produce record floods throughout the Valley, and NWS made its historic forecast: The river would crest at 47.5-49 feet in Grand Forks.

The height "49 feet" became a mantra, as volunteers worked for weeks sandbagging and building to match that height.

In March came more snow, and in April, sandbagging and levee building began in earnest in greater Grand Forks— even during a blizzard. On April 4, a final blizzard, "Hannah" (so named by the *Grand Forks Herald*, which popularized the practice of naming blizzards just as hurricanes are named), delivered the deathblow, bringing freezing rain and 20 inches of snow and leaving 300,000 people without power. On the same day Hannah arrived, the Red River reached 28 feet in Grand Forks—official flood stage.

Flooding began in the southern portion of the Red. First, during the weekend of April 4-6, more than a quarter of the population of Breckenridge, Minn. evacuated, and 500 buildings there were damaged. President Clinton declared the region a federal disaster area.

As the waters flowed north, the residents of Grand Forks watched their neighbors to the south. Flood fighters in Fargo fought valiantly, and the city escaped major damage. (The Fargo city engineer later commented to the *Grand Forks Herald:* "We spent a lot of money being lucky.")

On April 7, for the second time in a year, President Clinton declared North Dakota a federal disaster area. In Fargo-Moorhead April 11, the Red River reached its highest level there in 100 years, cresting at 37.61 feet. On that day, NWS predicted the river would crest in Grand Forks the week of April 20.

With their eye on the calendar and "49" on their minds, Grand Forks residents and volunteers from neighboring states sandbagged, working day and night, focused on saving their city and their homes. They watched the river rise, at a rate of an inch an hour, 2 feet a day, in the days leading up to the flooding, working feverishly.

By April 14, the river had risen to 44.43 feet, and it was only then that the NWS raised its crest prediction to 50 feet. Two days later, NWS raised the bar again, to 50.5, then to 51.5 and 53 and 54 feet. But by then, it was too late for people to do anything but give up and evacuate.

A 2007 Minnesota Public Radio story recalls the despair residents and city officials felt when they realized what was about to happen: "Former Grand Forks Mayor Pat Owens says the night she ordered a citywide evacuation lingers like a bad dream. There are images she can't forget, like a city engineer asking forgiveness because the dikes he built failed to hold back floodwater. 'I'll never forget that because he had tears running down his face and he was a good-sized guy,' recalls Owens."

On April 18, the Red reached 52.62 feet, rising 18 inches in 18 hours. That night, dikes failed throughout Grand Forks, and with civil defense sirens sounding, officials evacuated 47,500 people.

In a PBS interview during this period, North Dakota Sen. Byron Dorgan (D) said: "This is sort of a slow-motion disaster. You know, most of the time a tornado hits, and it's over, or an earthquake. We're going to see a crest probably tonight in Grand Forks, and it'll be around for five, six days. And it'll be weeks before people get back into their homes."

On April 19, the Red reached 52.89 feet in Grand Forks. Ice-cold river water poured into the city; water was four feet deep in downtown Grand Forks when fire broke out in the Security Building there, damaging or destroying 11 buildings on three city blocks. Ironically, the flood waters prevented firefighters from dousing the flames, which stood 25 feet high, according to observers. The excess water on the ground blocked firetrucks from getting to the burning buildings. The office of the *Grand Forks Herald* was among the casualties, and 120 years of archived history was destroyed. It was a horrific scene watched in news footage around the world, fire and water mixing in a devastating symbol of disaster.

The Herald's editor, Mike Jacobs, said in a KTCA-TV interview during the flood: "It's an unimaginable event. I mean, this has not ever happened ... we had all the science, we had all the predictions, we had all the elevation maps, you know. We were out there. We literally wore ourselves out. I mean, I still hurt from sandbagging. You know, we wore ourselves out, and we knew we were going to win because we've always won before. And it just didn't occur to us that the river has that kind of power."

Unbelievably, the displaced *Grand Forks Herald* did not miss a single day of publication, coming out with the headline after the fire: "Come hell and high water." The newspaper staff operated out of a grade school in nearby Manvel, covering the flood that destroyed their homes. *St. Paul Pioneer Press*—a sister Knight-Ridder newspaper— provided newsroom space and staff.

The Red River crested in Grand Forks at 54.35 feet on April 21. Water spread out over two miles away from the river. All of East Grand Forks and 90 percent of Grand Forks residents were evacuated—East Grand Forks residents to nearby Crookston (especially at the University of Minnesota Crookston), and 3,000 Grand Forks residents to the Grand Forks Air Force Base, and thousands of others to motels, shelters and homes nearby and throughout the country. The city's water supply was exhausted. *The Herald* kept residents connected, publishing at temporary sites for a year, and dropping papers by plane or trucking papers to nearby towns where pockets of residents sought shelter. It is little wonder the paper won the 1998 Pulitzer Prize for public service.

Cities to the north, including Winnipeg, suffered some flood damage, but nothing like the devastation in Grand Forks and East Grand Forks.

The river began to recede April 22 in Grand Forks, but on that flat land, the water did not fall below flood stage until May 19. Because of that, many homeowners could not visit their damaged property until May. An estimated 83 percent (9,001) of Grand Forks homes and 62 percent (761) of the city's commercial units were damaged.

Most schools were destroyed, and classes were cancelled for the rest of the year in Grand Forks and East Grand Forks. (But not prom. Two months after the flood, alternative rock band Soul Asylum played at the joint prom held for local high school students. The event took place in a hangar at Grand Forks Air Force Base. In 2004, the band released a live album of the concert, *After the Flood: Live from the Grand Forks Prom, June 28, 1997.*)

Joan Kroc, the McDonald's heiress, anonymously donated $15 million to be divided equally among each damaged household. Others pitched in, too, by the thousands. In the four months following the flood, nearly 20,000 volunteers total came to Grand Forks to help clean up the 60 million tons of flood debris that eventually was hauled to landfills. An estimated $2 billion in damage was sustained in Grand Forks and East Grand Forks.

All the while, the National Weather Service took a beating for its six-week-long crest prediction of 49 feet in Grand Forks. The five-foot discrepancy between the actual crest and the original forecast angered residents whose homes were destroyed, especially after they had worked for weeks to meet the 49-foot level. Echoing the sentiments of many, one homeowner spray-painted "49 feet my ass" on his flood-damaged home.

The National Weather Service has improved its forecasting methods since 1997. Some of what they learned simply involves publicizing the uncertainties of their predictions. In the paper "Who Decides? Forecasts and Responsibilities in the 1997 Red River Flood," scientist Roger A. Pielke Jr. analyzed the use and misuse of flood forecasts in the 1997 flood, and offered conclusions about river forecasting, including:

• The NWS needs to better understand the uncertainty in its own outlooks and forecasts.

• The NWS needs to explore how to better communicate uncertainty to decision-makers. Misuse of predictions can lead to greater costs than if no prediction were provided.

• Local decision-makers need to explore ways to become more forecast-independent.

• Responsibility for flood flight decision-making belongs at the local level.

• Focus more attention on understanding the actual use and misuse of predictions.

In January 2007, a $409 million flood protection project for Grand Forks and East Grand Forks was completed. The project—the first of its kind in the country—includes a series of floodwalls, earthen levees, flood pumping stations, storm sewers, diversion ditches and recreational areas. The first test of the facility came in April 2006, when the Red River reached the fifth-highest crest ever recorded in Grand

Forks (47.85 inches). With the flood protection project nearly complete, for the first time at a river level that high, no sandbagging was needed, and the city sustained no damage.

Grand Forks and East Grand Forks have taken pride in "rebuilding bigger, better and stronger," just as former Grand Forks Mayor Pat Owens called for. It's a victory, to be sure, and most citizens stayed, even after losing everything. But ultimately, inhabitants of the area remain at the mercy of the Valley's oldest resident—the Red River—just as their ancestors before them:

"Immigrants to the Northern Plains took just over a century to change the river that forms North Dakota's eastern border," according to *North Dakota Water Magazine*. "They took its wild winding ways and altered it into an agricultural and industrial workhorse. But the Red still rebels back to its ancient character when it viciously attacks with floods and decidedly deserts the valley's inhabitants during droughts. The Red is the heart and heartache of the Red River Valley."

The town of Halstad, Minn., lies virtually isolated by a sea of flood water from the Red River Friday, April 18, 1997. (photo: AP/Jim Mone)

Conservation Officer Keith Backer patrols an area of East Grand Forks, Minn., via boat April 29, 1997. Ten years later, heavy rain and snow still make people nervous but a dike system has helped ease some fears. (photo: AP/Eric Gay)

Homes in East Grand Forks, Minn., underwater Saturday, April 26, 1997.
(photo: AP/David J. Phillip)

About 80 head of cattle are stranded on a dirt county road just north of Halstad, Minn., Saturday, April 19, 1997, as flood waters from the Red River force them from their grazing land. Their owner, Paul Vicker, had to bring feed to them by boat.
(photo: AP/Carolyn Kaster)

Smoke and flames rise from the Security Building Saturday, April 19, 1997, in Grand Forks, N.D. just hours after the rampaging Red River flooded the downtown area. Firefighters were unable to battle the blaze due to flooded streets.
(photo: AP/*St. Paul Pioneer Press*, John Doman)

The Kennedy Bridge, which connects Grand Forks, N.D., and East Grand Forks, Minn., was closed due to the flood waters Sunday, April 20, 1997. Most of the residents in both towns had evacuated. (photo: AP/David J. Phillip)

Dale Pesch holds onto a cat he rescued from his brother-in-law's home as he is boated out of East Grand Forks, Minn., Monday, April 21, 1997, during the flooding. Driving the boat is Terry Hofland. (photo: AP/John Gaps III)

Abandoned cars were submerged in downtown East Grand Forks, Minn., Friday, April 25, 1997, as the waters of the nearby Red River slowly receded. (photo: AP/John Gaps III)

The Blizzard of 2007
In Like a Lion

In somebody's garden there are tulip bulbs under the snowdrifts
quietly waiting.

–Duluth resident writing in on *Duluth News Tribune*
message board, March 2, 2007

It was weirdly warm in Minnesota as we rang in the new year
of 2007. After a fall that boasted 80-degree days in October,
a Thanksgiving in the 50s and a December barren of snow,
there was mumbling of El Niño and global warming. We're
accustomed to breaking winter weather records in Minnesota.
We *like* breaking those records, taking perverse pioneer pride
in living in places that boast of the country's record lows. But
the records that January were for high temperatures, and it was
unsettling. International Falls hit 41 degrees in January. Thin
ice in Minnesota's lakes ruined ice-skating plans, skiing events
and ice-fishing tournaments. Winter was AWOL around here.

For a second consecutive season, organizers of the St.
Paul Winter Carnival struggled with warm temperatures. (How
do you keep ice from melting on a balmy January day?) Even
the *New York Times* covered the story of the Winter Carnival's
plight: "Lake Phalen, from which the 2,500 giant, 400-pound
blocks of ice to build the maze are usually cut, just wasn't
frozen enough. ... The carnival planners suggested using clear
plastic, but public opposition was vigorous. They settled briefly
on large, ice-coated blocks of packed snow—introducing the

In March 2007 wind, snow and cold combined to make snow drift sculptures in Duluth.
(photo: courtesy Marcia Hales)

word 'snice' into the popular vocabulary. And then—good luck. Thickly frozen H2O was discovered on a Minneapolis lake that had been cleared of snow long enough to freeze harder than other nearby waters. Finally the weather turned colder, and St. Paul breathed a sigh of relief."

Still, for the first three weeks of February, much of Minnesota reported little or no snow. All that changed the last weekend of February when a major winter storm traveled through the Upper Midwest and deposited heavy snowfall. Southeastern Minnesota reported over two feet of new snow Feb. 23–26, and the entire state was blanketed with snow of at least six inches in the multi-day event. More than 140 Minnesota school districts canceled classes.

Then, as if to prove the first storm was no fluke (and with National Weather Service meteorologist Byron Paulson forecasting, unceremoniously, "We're going to get pummeled"), snow began to fall, again. While Minnesotans still tried to work out where to put the snow from the first storm, along came another powerful winter blast that dumped a foot or more of snow across southern Minnesota, the Twin Cities and along the North Shore. Strong winds led to blizzard conditions in Duluth and across western Minnesota. Temperatures plummeted. Many northern Minnesota cities hit -30 F or lower during the cold snap, according to a March 2007 newsletter by the State Climatology Office.

From extreme temperatures of 54 degrees at Lamberton in Redwood County on Feb. 21, to -42 degrees at Embarrass in St. Louis County on March 4—our Minnesota winter bragging rights had returned, with a vengeance.

Hardest hit by the storm was Duluth, where "the 2007 blizzard" brought over 20 inches of snow and winds exceeding 60 mph. According to the National Weather Service in Duluth: "The storm began taking shape on Wednesday, Feb. 28, as a large and strong upper level trough moved into the central United States. As a result, surface low pressure developed over the Oklahoma and Texas panhandles. The surface low moved east across northern Oklahoma Wednesday evening, then to eastern Iowa by Thursday morning and to eastern Wisconsin by Friday."

And then came the snow, in two separate waves. First in areas from Hinckley to Hayward, then across the Iron Range. Winds picked up, and there were whiteout conditions along the North Shore. "But the worst of the wind was still to come. The most intense part of the storm began mid-afternoon Thursday and continued through the night," according to a National Weather Service report. "Snow fell at rates of 1 to 2 inches per hour, accompanied by sustained winds of 40 mph, with frequent gusts above 50 mph. The most severe conditions were within 10 to 20 miles of Lake Superior, including Two Harbors, Duluth and Cloquet. Duluth and Superior pulled snow plows off the roads by late afternoon, and travel became virtually impossible as sustained winds increased to 40-50 mph with gusts over 60 mph."

Wind gusts of 66 mph were recorded at Duluth Sky Harbor Airport, with reports of even stronger winds elsewhere in town. In Duluth, it was a classic, full-blown Minnesota blizzard. That city had seen its share of 20-inch snowstorms. But winds that whip up whiteouts and roof-high snowdrifts are notable. Duluth's Park Point neighborhood on Minnesota Point was cut off for some 17 hours. Winds were reported at 67 miles per hour there Thursday night just as snow was its heaviest. Conditions were so bad the point was sealed off, with gates blocking traffic at Duluth's aerial lift bridge.

According to Park Point resident Catharine Larsen, writing later in Duluth's *Budgeteer:* "We were at the total mercy of Mother Nature during the blizzard. On Park Point at least, there were sustained wind gusts of 60 mph. I couldn't believe what we were witnessing. Slowly, but surely, we saw our house grow darker and darker as the doors and the windows were covered in snow. They closed Park Point for the day and night of the blizzard."

On its website, The Inn on Lake Superior reported after the storm: "The snow drifts in our backyard went up to our second floor balconies! Canal Park was closed down on Thursday, March 1st as a major blizzard came through with extreme winds of 55 mph coming off Lake Superior. All Canal Park restaurants closed early on Thursday afternoon in preparation for the storm so finding something to eat became close to impossible. Always prepared, the Inn on Lake Superior had chili for the guests who were stranded with us."

Conditions prevented the *Duluth News Tribune* from delivering Friday's paper, a rare occurence. But the paper's website kept readers connected. The paper's message board on March 2 was typical Minnesota storm-day banter:

Gary L. at 10:09 a.m.—I love this. I remember a storm back in the early-'80s that buried cars. It was nice to sit and watch the storm.

Joe K: at 10:09 a.m.—COULD SOMEONE PLEASE PLOW SUPERIOR STREET THIS MORNING!!

Loren K. at 7:20 a.m.—From what I've seen of this storm so far it's just a puppy. Why back when I was a kid now we had blizzards and so on and so forth … and school was five miles away … and up hill too!

Beryl K. at 7:20 a.m.— Think of it this way… In somebody's garden there are tulip bulbs under the snowdrifts quietly waiting…

Joe N. at 11:46 a.m.— Stay home! It's very unsafe for anything to be open today and Friday. Businesses should close now and let people go home!!! Does the term blizzard mean anything to you. People die in blizzards. Is that worth another dollar?

Tim Z. at 9:48 a.m.—Sled, snowmobile … that simple.

Scott M. at 9:48 a.m.—People need to get a life and be real. Going crazy at the grocery store for a possible one-day shut down? Are these people going to starve??? Come on, we live in the Northland!

"It's a whale of a storm," Gov. Tim Pawlenty summarized on his Friday, March 2, morning radio show.

Indeed, much of the Twin Cities got a foot of snow, with western suburbs reporting as much as 18 inches. In northern Minnesota, Finland reported 25 inches, and Duluth 19.8 inches. The toughest conditions Friday were in southern Minnesota. With blizzard warnings in effect, Interstate 35 from Albert Lea south to Ames, Iowa, closed, frustrating stranded travelers and truckers. Interstate 90 west to Sioux Falls, S.D., was also closed.

It was fitting timing for Duluth National Weather Service meteorologist Sam Standfield. That Friday was the final day of his 32-year career. "This is probably the way to go out,"

Standfield told the *Star Tribune*. "You get a few events like this in your career, and they're pretty memorable." Standfield and his wife then moved to Washington state.

But in the scope of Minnesota blizzards, this one was not devastating. Minnesota has a long history of March snowstorms, including a bad one in Duluth in March 1892. According to the *Duluth Daily Tribune* back then: "The blizzard of Wednesday, March 9, 1892, began about 4 a.m. with snow and winds of around 30 miles per hour. By 3:30 p.m. the winds were clocked at 60 miles per hour, and four feet of snow had fallen by dawn on Thursday. Streetcar service was suspended after noon on Wednesday because of snow accumulating on the tracks—even with the new electric rotary snowplow trying to clear it. ... Snow drifts of twenty feet formed on the north side of Superior Street, forcing business owners to tunnel through the snow to get to their doorways."

Still, there is something celebratory about a Minnesota blizzard. When lives are spared and school is out, joyful cries of "snow day!" ring across the frozen land. It's a shout not limited to children. From the March 2, 2007 blog on www.mnspeak.com came this entry:

"I'm a Saint Paul Public teacher. First snow day since 2002 and on a Friday, no less! Thank God the Saint Paul bars didn't close for the snow."

Trees were unable to withstand the weight of the heavy snow.
(photo: courtesy Marcia Hales)

Drifts overwhelmed a house on Park Point in Duluth.
(photo: courtesy Marcia Hales)

The day after the blizzard, Duluth streets were lined with March snow.
(photo: courtesy Marcia Hales)

With downtown Duluth in the background, ice gathered on the shore of Lake Superior in Park Point. (photo: courtesy Marcia Hales)

The Flash Floods of 2007
From Drought to Downpour

Blizzard, flood, drought and fire. In the first half of 2007, Minnesotans had seen it all: unseasonably warm temperatures, a statewide blizzard in early-March and flooding in Browns Valley on the South Dakota border, which caused evacuation of 100 people March 13. Then talk turned to the ongoing drought, carried over from 2006, with the State Climatology Office reporting in early spring that northern Minnesota was in extreme and severe drought conditions, central Minnesota in moderate drought and the rest of the state abnormally dry.

By May 5, with these dry conditions and abnormally warm air temperatures, most of the state was in high fire danger when a fire started at the edge of the Boundary Waters Canoe Area Wilderness near Ham Lake. Flames spread quickly through the parched forests, fanned by strong winds. Before long, a massive wildfire raged through the BWCAW, burning for 21 days and forcing hundreds to evacuate. Some 50,000 acres burned, destroying more than 130 structures, including 62 houses. It was a heartbreaking time for residents who loved their wilderness, with lasting repercussions. Months later, from Voyageur Canoe Outfitter's website came this blog: "Every time I see a tree that was burned or a vacant lot where a house once stood I can't help but think of the terror that enveloped all of us for days on end. The fear of losing our homes, possessions, trees, lives or livelihood, it was a lot to process. The flames

Rushford, Minn. underwater in the flood of 2007. (photo: courtesy Peggi Redalen)

popping up everywhere; alongside the road, next to homes and in my favorite forested areas. The sense of loss, the changing wilderness that will never be the same in my lifetime."

In summer, dry conditions remained throughout the state—sometimes devastatingly so. It was the worst Minnesota drought since 1988, with some experts citing comparisons to the Dust Bowl days. Crop conditions deteriorated. Water levels in lakes and rivers had sunk to record lows. By July, Lake Superior was roughly 20 inches below normal, according to the U.S. Army Corps of Engineers, forcing ships to lighten cargo loads to make it in and out of port.

By August, with much of southern, central and northeastern Minnesota in moderate to severe drought conditions, Minnesota Sen. Norm Coleman (R) requested emergency assistance for farmers in 25 drought-stricken Minnesota counties. "This unrelenting drought continues to adversely affect over three-fourths of our great state," said Coleman. "This financial assistance comes as a relief to the entire state as the rural communities that have been affected play a large role in sustaining Minnesota's economy, food supply and overall way of life."

On Aug. 1, all talk of weather, and everything else, stopped as the world learned, along with Minnesotans, the horrific news of the 35W bridge collapsing into the Mississippi River in Minneapolis, claiming 13 lives and injuring 100. President George Bush came to Minneapolis, pledging aid and support, and later, declaring the site a federal disaster area.

While Minnesotans still grieved, grappling with the unreality of the bridge collapse, tragedy struck again in southeastern Minnesota when, in the midst of a drought, historic rainfall descended, causing more loss of life.

Even as farmers prayed for relief for failing crops, forecasts for Aug. 18 called for heavy rain in central and southern Minnesota. And rain it did—in a series of thunderstorms Aug 18 through 20 that caused widespread flash flooding. By the time it was over, Dodge, Fillmore, Houston, Olmsted, Steele, Wabasha and Winona counties were declared federal disaster areas. Seven people were killed in flood-related incidents—five in Winona, two in Houston. Thousands were evacuated, and thousands of others had retained damage to homes and businesses in what State Sen. Sharon Erickson Ropes called "the worst disaster that's hit southeast Minnesota in a lifetime." At least $67 million in damage was estimated.

The historic storm set a state record for rainfall during a 24-hour period: 15.10 inches of rain in Hokah (in Houston County, on the eastern state line), which broke the old record of 10.84 inches. An unofficial 24-hour total of over 17 inches was recorded near Caledonia. The highest total for the entire event was 18.17 inches near La Crescent. The storm produced the heaviest rain concentrated in a line running from Claremont and Rochester to La Crosse, Wis.

Southeastern Minnesota is in land called "the Driftless Area," which was not covered by the last glacier, leaving the soil thin and less able to retain water; flash floods are prone to happen here. And indeed flooding, mud slides and road closures were numerous throughout the area. In Brownsville, eight people survived as their houses were pushed over a bluff by a mud slide, according to the *Winona Daily News*. Amtrak train service between Minneapolis and La Crosse was shut down for a week because of damage to the tracks.

In Fillmore County, the city of Rushford was completely surrounded by water. The city was evacuated and all roads in and out of town were closed. There was no gas, phones or electricity. The sewage plant was contaminated. St. Joseph's church in Rushford, the only church in town not affected by flooding, became the central relief center for that city. The parish served 1,500 meals a day for weeks after the flooding to flood victims and recovery workers such as the National Guard, building inspectors and county work crews. The *Fillmore County Journal* described the onset of the flood there:

"Residents know that right around 3 a.m., cold brown water full of tree parts and barrels and tires and chunks of crumbled concrete breached the top of Rush Creek levee. Still rising as it came over the dike, water crashed down like Niagara Falls on houses and cars and families living on the so-called 'dry side' of the dikes."

In Winona County, the Red Cross estimated 6,375 families were affected by flooding. All county roads were closed. Portions of Winona were evacuated, and citizens were moved to St. Mary's College, Lewiston and Caledonia. In Houston County, the city of Houston was evacuated, and the city was without power. Later, a Houston resident wrote in a blog on the flood-relief website www.rootrelief.org:

"It has been humbling to live through this surge of nature. Driving around, seeing the utter destruction and trying to grasp the whole picture, it is impossible. Landscapes that I have known my entire life are unfamiliar. The sense of comfort and security the surrounding hills once gave is quickly turned to isolation and anxiety when the forecast calls for rain. We are living in and adapting to a new world. The reaching out of strangers, neighbors, family and friends allows 'things happen for a reason' to creep into my mind. What an experience. In life, there truly are no guarantees."

Gov. Tim Pawlenty ordered 240 National Guard soldiers to the area to help. The Army Corps of Engineers opened up the floodgates on the rising Root River to release some of the water creating pressure on the dike in Houston. With seven counties declared federal disaster areas, the path was clear for federal aid to flow into southeastern Minnesota. But federal funds would not be nearly enough. Much more would be needed, and flood victims soon began calling for help from state government. Editorials in southeastern Minnesota newspapers reflected the region's collective impatience as they waited for Gov. Pawlenty to call a special session of the Legislature to approve and release disaster aid. According to the Aug. 27, 2007 *Winona Daily News:*

This year, it is southeast Minnesota left reeling, but in other years, in other seasons it has been Mankato, St. Peter, Moorhead and East Grand Forks that felt the devastation of Minnesota's wild weather.

The only prediction that we can safely make is that our region, our communities will not be the last and, hard as it is to believe today, probably will not even be the hardest hit.

Minnesota deserves—Minnesota needs—more than a piecemeal approach to disaster relief. It is time for the Legislature to not only deal with the immediate crisis, but put in place the legislative mechanisms that provide fast, effective relief to be brought to disaster-stricken Minnesotans whenever, wherever lives are disrupted and homes and businesses are destroyed.

Pawlenty called a special session on Sept. 10, and after a record seven hours, the Minnesota Legislature released a $157 million package of relief funding to flood-ravaged southeastern Minnesota. Called the "fastest and largest disaster response bill on record" for Minnesota, the bill included provisions for:

• repairing flood-damaged sewer and water systems, city and county buildings, municipal utilities and state and local parks;

• grants and loans to small businesses;

• low-interest and forgivable loans to individual homeowners;

• property tax abatements for flooded homes and businesses;

• funds to clean up and repair schools and provide aid to offset pupils who left school districts after the flood.

The bill also provided more than $5 million in aid to Minnesotans affected by weather earlier in the year— farmers plagued by the drought, those affected by forest fire damage in the BWCAW, and victims of flooding in Browns Valley and Crookston.

In the weeks after the Southeastern Minnesota flood, with government promises secured, neighbors turned to the real work of helping one another. Fundraisers were plentiful throughout the region. At the Rochester International Event

Center, there was the "Life Vest" fundraiser, where attendees could gather to hear country, rock and jazz bands in a one-day event, with proceeds going to the Red Cross to benefit flood victims. At the Back 40 Supper Club (formerly Elmer's) in Caledonia, folks could listen to a live band and buy a chance to win a 50-inch plasma TV. In Houston, residents looked forward to the "Flood Relief Pancake Breakfast" sponsored by Houston Public Schools.

It's what people here do. It's what they have come to rely on, even when they move away:

"Living so far away from family makes situations like this very difficult," wrote a former Hokah resident, now living in Washington, D.C., on the www.rootrelief.org website. "I'd first like to thank my family that's still local for pulling together and helping our parents ... when their home was destroyed by the mud slide. Next, I'd like to extend my sincere appreciation to the community of Hokah for the incredible outpouring of support and assistance. We heard today that the children of St. Peter's school are taking lunch to Mom and Dad every day. They are currently living in a house loaned to them from another very generous Hokahite across the street from the church. It's very comforting to know our parents are nestled in such an incredibly supportive and giving community."

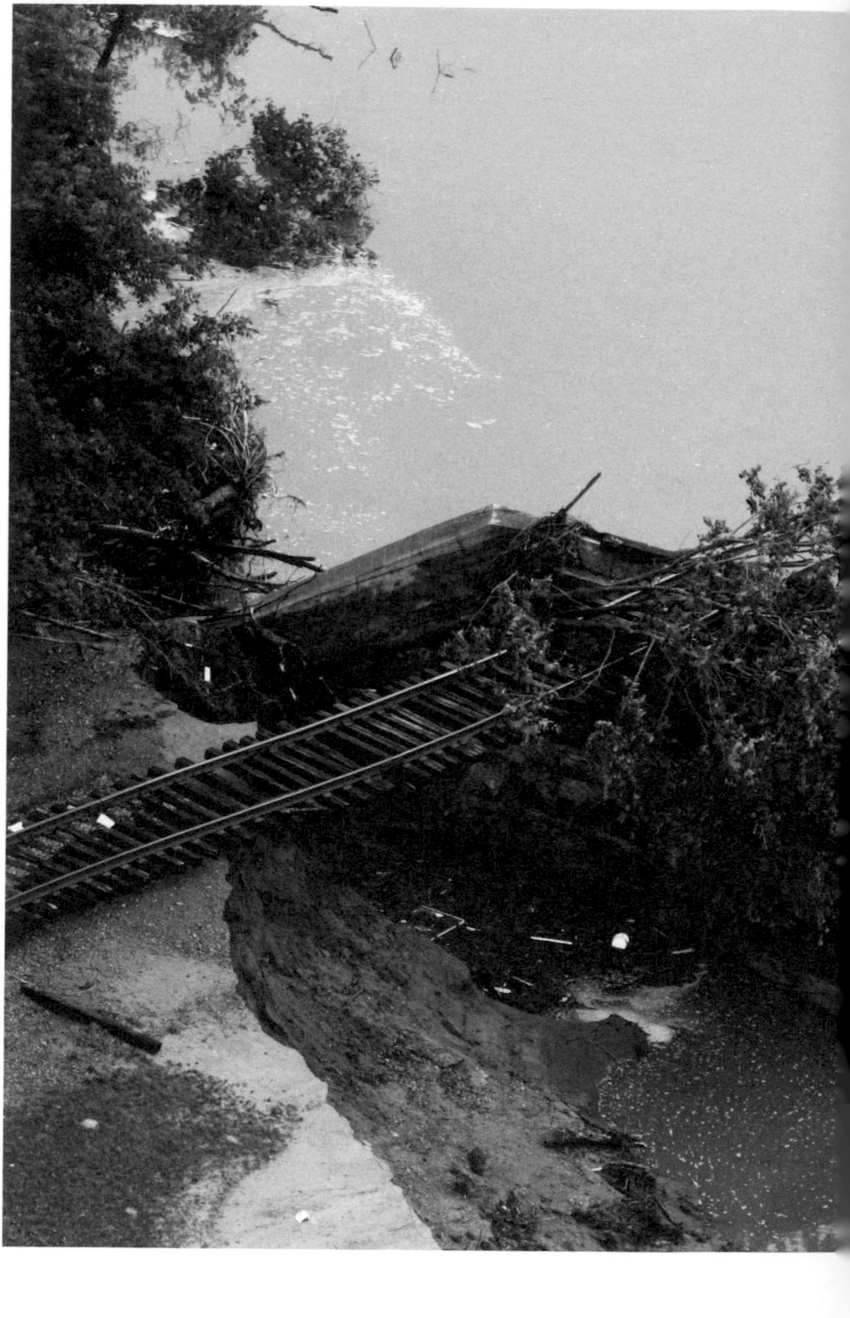

Railroad tracks washed out near Winona after the August 2007 downpours and flooding.
(photo: Associated Press)

A trailer sits atop a pickup truck in a flood-ravaged campground near Houston, Minn. (photo: Associated Press)

This house landed on train tracks near Stockton during the August 2007 flooding.
(photo: Associated Press)

The earth gave way in this scene near Winona.
(photo: Associated Press)

Gov. Tim Pawlenty consults with Browns Valley residents during the flood.
(photo: Associated Press)

Churches and homes were leveled by the 1919 Fergus Falls tornado.
(photo: Minnesota Historical Society)

Top 20 Minnesota Weather Events of the 20th Century

The Minnesota State Climatology Office asked state climate experts to choose the five most significant Minnesota weather-driven events of the 20th Century. Voters were provided with a list of candidate events, but were encouraged to offer their own nominations. Here's what they chose:

1. 1930s Dust Bowl
2. 1940 Armistice Day Blizzard
3. 1991 Halloween Blizzard
4. 1997 Red and Minnesota River Flooding
5. 1965 Tornado Outbreak (tie)
5. 1965 Mississippi and Minnesota River Flooding (tie)
7. 1975 Storm that Sunk the Edmund Fitzgerald
8. 1987 Twin Cities Superstorm
9. 1988 Drought
10. 1993 Summer Flooding
11. 1998 St. Peter/Comfrey Tornadoes
12. 1975 Central Minnesota Blizzard
13. 1919 Fergus Falls Tornado
14. 1982 Metro Area Twin January Snowstorms
15. 1976 Drought
16. 1992 Chandler Tornado
17. 1904 Twin Cities Tornadoes and Windstorms
18. 1992 Cold and Wet Spring
19. 1934 May Dust Storm
20. 1948 Winona Windstorm

Drawings and photos depict damage from the 1883 Rochester tornado.

The 1883 Rochester Tornado

On July 21, 1883 in southeast Minnesota, two large tornadoes struck—one an F4 that killed four people near Dodge Center, 15 miles west of Rochester. One month later, on Aug. 21, an F5 tornado moved through Rochester, killing 37 in the area and injuring 200. Some 135 homes were destroyed, another 200 damaged. Many of the residents who survived the tornado said the enormous roar of the approaching storm warned them. It was one in a series of tornadoes that hit southeast Minnesota that day.

Rochester did not have a place to treat the injured from this tornado, as there were only three hospitals in Minnesota outside of the Twin Cities at that time, none near Rochester. So a Rochester dance hall was transformed into a temporary emergency room. Doctor William Mayo and his two sons, William and Charles, took charge of caring for the injured, along with Mother Mary Alfred Moes and the Sisters of St. Francis.

After this disaster, the Mayos and the sisters realized the need for a hospital in Rochester. Collections were gathered, and in 1889 Saint Mary's hospital was built. It was later renamed Mayo Clinic.

—Source: Wikipedia, National Weather Service

The Weatherball was a familiar sight in the Twin Cities skyline from 1949 to 1982.
(photo: Minnesota Historical Society)

Remembering the Weatherball

Once upon a time, weather forecasting was much simpler in the Twin Cities. Between 1949 and 1982, if you were wondering about the weather and were within 15 miles of downtown Minneapolis, all you need do was look to the skyline and to the 12-story Weatherball perched atop the Northwestern National Bank building at 600 Marquette Ave., observe the color of the ball, and sing the snappy jingle (which everyone knew):

> *When the Weatherball is red, warmer weather is ahead.*
> *When the Weatherball is green, no change in weather is foreseen.*
> *When the Weatherball is white, colder weather is in sight.*
> *If colors blink by night or day, precipitation's on the way.*

Built to withstand winds of up to 140 miles per hour, the Weatherball (hailed as the tallest illuminated sign between Chicago and the West Coast) survived hurricane-force gales just three days after it began operating in 1949.

In the 1950s and '60s the Weather Bureau called the bank with the day's forecast and bank staff programed the ball accordingly. In the '70s and early-'80s the Weather Service staff at the airport controlled the ball via keypad and verified the ball's color with binoculars.

A fire on Thanksgiving Day 1982 destroyed the bank building, and the Weatherball was moved to the Minnesota State Fairgrounds in St. Paul. In 2000, it was discovered the Weatherball had deteriorated beyond repair, and it was destroyed.

If it's Playoff Time, There's a Storm Brewing

I f it's a championship playoff year for the Minnesota Twins
or Vikings, you'd best keep your eyes on the sky. There's a
good chance a storm is brewing that year. Take a look back:

Year	Playoff	Storm Event
1965	Twins World Series	1965 Flooding, Twin Cities Tornadoes
1975	Vikings Super Bowl	Super Bowl Blizzard
1987	Twins World Series	Twin Cities Superstorm
1991	Twins World Series	Halloween Blizzard

The 1965 Minnesota Twins.

Top, the 1975 Minnesota Vikings. Below, Kent Hrbek and the Twins celebrate in 1987.
(photos: courtesy Minnesota Twins and Minnesota Vikings)

Cold Enough For Ya?

The lowest temperature ever recorded in Minnesota was -60 F, recorded on Feb. 2, 1996 at Tower.

The highest temperature ever recorded in Minnesota is 114 F. This record high was recorded on July 6, 1936, at Moorhead, tying a record set in Beardsley in 1917.

(photo: courtesy Marcia Hales, Duluth, MN)

Looking Back

Storms!

If you enjoyed *Storms 2*, make sure to read *Storms!*–the book that launched The Minnesota Series–which includes chapters about these memorable Minnesota weather events:

The Armistice Day Blizzard of 1940.

The great floods of April 1965.

The storm that sunk the **Edmund Fitzgerald**, Nov. 10, 1975.

The "Television Tornado," July 1986.

The rain superstorm in the Twin Cities, July 1987.

The Halloween Blizzard of 1991.

The St. Peter Tornado, March 29, 1988.

The Boundary Waters Blowdown, July 4, 1999.

Also look for these books available now in The Minnesota Series:

Music Legends–A Rewlnd on the Minnesota Music Scene

Media Tales–Stories of Minnesota TV, Radio, Publications and Personalities

Available at stores throughout Minnesota and online at www.minnesotaseries.com

About the Author

Sheri O'Meara

Sheri O'Meara is editor of The Minnesota Series, co-author of *Storms!* and *Media Tales* and will be co-author of the next book, *Famous Crimes*. She is also currently editor of *Minnesota Meetings and Events* magazine and has served as founding editor of monthly publications for K102-FM (where she was recognized by *Billboard* magazine for her work on *Minnesota Country* magazine), Sun Country Airlines and SimonDelivers. As editor of *Format Magazine*, she covered Minnesota's advertising and media industries for 10 years, the magazine receiving a Crystal Clarion Award from Minnesota Women in Communications. She has managed magazines for organizations including The Guthrie Theater and Minnesota Orchestra, and has written for a variety of Twin Cities publications. Sheri is also lead singer in the Twin Cities-based Celtic band Locklin Road.

Back cover photo: Snow reached the top of power poles in Willmar in 1965.
(photo: Minnesota Historical Society)

Coming Up

Famous Crimes

In the next edition of The Minnesota Series, revisit the intriguing crimes from Minnesota's historic past and modern era, including:

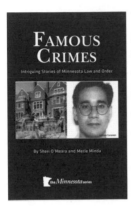

The legendary **James-Younger gang's** daring Northfield raid.

The famous **Congdon mansion** murders.

The mysterious **Virginia Piper** kidnapping.

The notorious **Andrew Cunanan.**

The infamous gangsters of prohibition-era St. Paul.

The case of **Lois Jurgens.**

The murder of **Carol Thompson** ... and much more.

Don't miss this look back at some of Minnesota's most famous cases of law and order!

Also watch for:

Political Stars

From famous families–(the Mondales, Humphreys and Colemans) to the "Rudys" (Perpich and Boschwitz) to Minnesota's first congresswoman (Coya Knutson) to our most colorful governor ever (Jesse Ventura)–Minnesota politicians make for the most remarkable stories.

Don't miss these engaging tales as well as the inside stories of Eugene McCarthy, Paul Wellstone, Al Franken and others!